Great Britain Parliament

A Brief and Impartial Review of the State of Great Britain

at the commencement of the session of 1783, humbly addressed to the

Right Honourable and Honourable the Lords and Commons of Great

Britain

Great Britain Parliament

A Brief and Impartial Review of the State of Great Britain
at the commencement of the session of 1783, humbly addressed to the Right Honourable and Honourable the Lords and Commons of Great Britain

ISBN/EAN: 9783337195687

Printed in Europe, USA, Canada, Australia, Japan

Cover: Foto ©ninafisch / pixelio.de

More available books at **www.hansebooks.com**

A BRIEF AND IMPARTIAL

R E V I E W

OF THE STATE OF

GREAT BRITAIN,

AT THE

COMMENCEMENT

OF THE

SESSION OF 1783:

HUMBLY ADDRESSED

TO THE RIGHT HONOURABLE AND HONOURABLE

THE

LORDS AND COMMONS

OF

GREAT BRITAIN.

—— Quod ſi exemeris ex Naturâ Rerum benevolentiæ Junctionem, nec Domus ulla, nec Urbs ſtare poterit; ne Agri quidem Cultus permanebit —— Quæ enim Domus tam ſtabilis, quæ tam firma Civitas eſt, quæ non Odiis atque Diſſidiis funditus poſſit everti?

CICERO.

THE THIRD EDITION CORRECTED.

L O N D O N:
Printed for J. DEBRETT, (Succeſſor to Mr. ALMON,)
oppoſite BURLINGTON-HOUSE, PICCADILLY.
M.DCC.LXXXIII.

A

BRIEF AND IMPARTIAL

REVIEW, &c.

THE hour of quiet and repofe is the feafon moft proper for cool and difpaffionate reflection. The alarm and hurry incident to bufy and eventful fcenes, and the turbulent paffions excited by a fufpenfion of hope and fear, in a ftate of extended and hazardous hoftility, difquailfy the mind for fuch attentive confideration of the commonwealth, as is neceffary, in order to enable a good citizen to act in the manner moft conducive to the folid and fubftantial interefts of his country. Such confideration is ufeful at all times, but more particularly fo in a period decifive of our future welfare.

B   Without

Without mature reflection, and a detailed
view of the ftate of public affairs, there is a danger that the honeft and unfufpecting will become dupes to the felfifh and defigning. It is
not my purpofe to queftion the degree of regard and reverence due, to that fpecies of public opinion, which is ufually termed the *voice
of the people*. But I cannot forbear to obferve,
that the true way to preferve its dignity and importance, is to render it the voice of truth and
juftice, and a fober difcretion. The voice of
the people ought never to be degraded to the
echo of revenge, difcontent and difappointed
ambition. To make the popular voice the juft
ftandard of public virtue, it is neceffary that it
fhould be the refult of minute inveftigation
and attentive enquiry. It will be contemned
and difregarded, when debafed to the inconftant
acclamation of inconfiderate temerity, or to the
idle clamour of mifguided folly. It cannot
therefore be an unprofitable tafk, to attempt
to enlighten the public mind, that the energy
of national opinion may be directed with effi-
cacy to promote the general welfare. This I
think, will be found more neceffary in the prefent, than in any paft time.

On setting out to the public view a plain state of our affairs, both foreign and domestic, it will be seen, that if there ever has been a season of peculiar emergence—a crisis of uncommon delicacy—If there has been, at any time, a conjuncture in the affairs of a nation that called for the collective wisdom, and united exertion of the whole body of the people, it is to be met with in the present situation of the British empire. It is the purpose of the present address, to collect into one point of view, the numerous difficulties and embarrassments, with which we are surrounded on every side; and to sketch out such a picture of our true situation, as will move every British heart and hand to co-operate in the great work of restoring us to our former prosperous state. The plan of *systematic discord* had a long trial, and most calamitous issue. Every good man wishes to see it buried in the same grave, where it has laid the grandeur and prosperity of his country.

It is something, that we have got a breathing time from our difficulties—It has been dearly purchased, and requires much management and address to turn it to account. In this pause of calamity, we have time to look around us, and contemplate the many new political relations,

which

which the indpendence of America has introduced. Many and great as the changes are, that
have been already produced by this revolution,
I hazard but little in pronouncing it pregnant
with events, ftill more numerous and important.

The difficulties are confiderable that attend
any fpeculation on a fubject, at once complicated and new. Hiftory furnifhes no lights to
guide us, in a conjuncture, to which nothing
parallel can be difcovered in the annals of mankind. The balance of power, which has exer-
cifed the talents, and agitated the paffions of the
European world, for near a century paft, is
now entirely deftroyed, and a frefh equilibrium
is to be fought after in the nice equipoife of new
divifions and fubdivifions of alliance, power,
jealoufy and competition. Were a new world
to have fprung up from the depths of the ocean,
flourifhing in men, arms, cultivation and commerce ; a more entire and complete reverfe of
the fyftem of European politics, could not have
been effected.

Nor is it the actual fituation of things, that
alone has been reverfed by the late revolution.
The opinions of mankind have undergone a
mighty

mighty change. All the fpeciousp laufibilities of the world have loft their authority. The minds of men unreftrained by the reverence due to ancient maxims, and eftablifhed ufage, are univerfally agitated with a bufy fpirit of change and innovation. Thofe, who are acquainted with the mighty influence of opinion in all human affairs, are not to be informed, what a large portion of political obedience depends upon its authority.

Retrofpective wifdom, and book knowledge, are little available in fuch a trying concurrence of difficulties—It requires a prompt fagacity to difcern the objects actually paffing in view, and to adapt our conduct to the exigency of the times, inftead of dully plodding on in the antiquated trammels of an exploded fyftem. It is not the leaft of her misfortunes, that Britain fhould be obliged to quit her ancient maxims, and be compelled, in her old age, to enter upon a new ftudy of experimental policy, where knowledge is to be gradually gleaned from laborious difcovery, independent of any known eftablifhed theory. An intimate acquaintance with the thoufand ways in which our remaining power and commerce are liable to be affected, by the fhifting impreffion of a new empire,

in

in a new world, is a fcene the moft abftrufe
and complicated.

This impreffion is felt in all quarters—In
our treaty with France, we find a ftipulation
for new commercial regulations— The fame in
the Spanifh treaty— The Dutch too, I mean
the ruling faction in Holland, feem but little
difpofed to renew the ancient connection which
has fubfifted between England and her, with
little exception, from the Revolution to the prefent time. Such are the fymptoms of change
abroad, created by American independence, while
in its domeftic affairs, England feels the fhock
to the very center of her commerce and power.
Can any man, who means honeftly to the commonwealth, think this a fit time for exafperat-
ing the bitternefs of internal divifion, and attempting a revival of paft animofities?

On a more diftinct view of our affairs, it will
evidently appear, that this general picture of
our difficulties and embarraffments, is, by no
means, overcharged. It will be preffed home
to the conviction and feeling of every man, that
to extricate us, is required not only a combi-
nation of whatever is left to this country, of
talents, of virtue, of perfonal weight and fa-

mily

mily confideration, in the higher orders; but alfo the chearful concurrence, and animating confidence of the people at large. To begin with our foreign politics.

France has been fo long in a ftate of conftant competition, and fo frequently of bitter hofti-lity with this country, as to be deemed, and generally ftiled, her natural enemy. The pro-priety of the phrafe may be an object of criti-cifm; but the juftnefs of the national feeling that originally gave birth to it, has feldom been queftioned. The *national* antipathy to France, is by no means founded on a *national* contrac-tion of fentiment; it originates from the necef-fary relation of things, and a ftrong fenfe of *national* intereft. Where two great ftates are fo fituated, as that the fecurity and power of the one are dependent on the weaknefs and de-preffion of the other—Where the gain of one is the lofs of the other—A fentiment of felf-prefervation, and, what is almoft equally for-cible in its operation—a fentiment of am-bition intolerant of equality, will for ever keep them in a ftate of fecret rivalfhip, or open hof-tility. France and England furnifh an example

in

in point. Ever fince the growth of the power
of France, by the union of her provinces, the
depreffion of the Houfe of Auftria, the weaknefs firft, and confequent acceffion of Spain,
and the creation of a formidable marine by
Lewis XIV. that power has proved a moft
dangerous neighbour to Great Britain. —
Nor will the competition ceafe, till a decided
fuperiority or an entire fubjugation of either
kingdom be fully accomplifhed.

To give an adequate view, therefore, of the
prefent ftate of our foreign politics, it will be
neceffary to confider our new relations to other
ftates, as they have a tendency to affect our
grand relation, to this our great and natural
rival, and in this confideration to look atten-
tively to the changes which commerce, the
great fource of power, has fuftained by the late
revolution. In purfuance of this plan, the moft
natural way is to begin with America, the great
original caufe of all the late and prefent alte-
rations.

It is painful to be obliged, at the outfet, to
confider America as an acceffion to the Houfe of
Bourbon. But that fuch an intimate union, political and commercial, as is highly detrimental

to

to this country, fubfifts at prefent between America and France, it is a truth univerfally obvious.

The political connection depends fo much
on caufes in their nature tranfient and temporary, and moulds in its very conftitution
fo many repelling principles, which the operation of a ftrong external neceffity has com-
preffed for a time into a forced union, that its
duration cannot be lafting. Its diffolution, however, muft be the work of time, and can be
very little accelerated by any efforts of ours.
On the contrary, any interpofition on our part
in the prefent jealoufy of the *New States*, and
during the obfequious dependence of Congrefs,
and the American agents, on the *liberality* of
France, would probably have a tendency the
very reverfe of what we hoped. Therefore,
great as is the preffure of the prefent evil, we
muft bear it with patience, and leave to time
the gradual but certain operation of the intrin-
fic caufes of difconnection, interwoven with the
French alliance. When the Americans are left
to themfelves, they will foon difcover a jealoufy of French influence, equally ftrong. as
their late impatience of Britifh fovereignty. In
the mean time, careffes and adulation can ferve
to no other end but to humble Great Britain,
and render America more fufpicious and lefs
practicable. Let us ftand with temper and

C   *firmnefs*

firmnefs on the fair ground of our right, and
adhere to the fpirit of treaty—America will
neither contemn nor fufpect us.

In regard to commerce, our minifters have
adopted what to me feems a very wife and politic meafure, and the only one immediately neceffary. I allude to the act of council prohibit-
ing all intercourfe, between the New States and
the Britifh Weft-India iflands. This meafure
deferves a good deal of confideration, both for
its own importance, as well as its having been
the object of much cenfure.

There is a degree of popular intoxication, infeparable from a great and fuccefsful revolution,
which, added to an infatuated facility on our firft
negociators, has mifled the Americans to think,
that they had been fighting, not merely for a
naked, barren independence, but an independence which was to be clothed, cherifhed and
foftered with all the tender care and fond fo-
licitude which, in the Halcyon days of former
connections, they had fo amply experienced.
The vaft range of important territory to which
the different colonies had fome pretenfions,
as Britifh fubjects; — the valuable fifheries
carried on in the fame right on the coafts of
Newfoundland;—an ifland difcovered, fettled,
and defended at an immenfe expence to this
country;

country;—the monopoly of the fur trade:—
All thefe enormous conceffions, which were
meant for conciliation, are confideᵣed by the
Americans, as fo many legal appurtenances to
inᵈependence. Is their gratitude called forth by
this extravagant profufion of kindnefs? Far
otherwife. The fact is, that while the policy of the Britifh government was lavifhing
commerce and territory on America; while
it was complimenting away, in all the re-
finement of a duplicity that ever recoils on
its author, Canada and the fifheries, the Americans were employed in meditating heavy
and unequal duties on the Britifh trade. While
the Britifh negociators are facrificing their
friends and allies,—the Loyalifts and the Indian nations;—while they are lavifhing the
commerce, dominion, marine, and good faith
of their country, on the *hope* of regaining the
American trade—the New States are employed
in fecuring to France the *jura amiciſſimæ gentis,*
in exclufion of Great Britain. I refer the reader
to the very difproportioned duties impofed by
America on the feveral articles of Englifh and
French Weft-India produce. They have lately
appeared in the daily papers, and therefore need
not be here repeated. But it is worthy of re-
mark, that thefe highly partial duties are in a
manner prohibitory of almoft the whole *export*
trade, from the Britifh iflands, to the American

continent. Obferve, then, the juftice of the
American complaints. They prohibit us from
the fale of *our* produce, the only benefit to be
expected, from *their* intercourfe, with the Britifh
Weft Indies. This lucrative part of the trade
they confine to the French; and yet they complain, that we preclude them from vending their
native commodities in the *Britifh* iflands.—
Modeft America! Unaffuming independence!—
Who, in the name of *reciprocity*, can refufe
fuch equitable demands?

What renders thefe pretenfions ftill more mor-
tifying, is, that they are urged in the high tone of
the *provifional articles*. A compliance with them
is not treated as matter of *favour* but of *right*.
Independence has been pretty well fledged by
the grants, which have been already made—The
Weft Indies are now demanded, to put it in
full feather. But the genius of conceffion no
longer predominates in the Britifh councils —
The policy of bartering folid advantages for
fpeculative returns of gratitude and affection is
now no more. The prefent minifters act on
plainer maxims; they are refolved to concede
nothing without a fuitable equivalent. This I
take to be the true ground of the late act of
council, which has been the fubject of fo much
prepofterous animadverfion.

What, in the name of wonder! will thefe clamorous advocates for unlimited indulgence to
the New States have us to do? Will they, with
an abject and ruinous complaifance, force on the
unrequiting fullennefs of independence, all the
long train of bounties, privileges, and exemp-
tions, in favour of American produce, with
which our ftatute book is loaded?—In return
for what? For an impracticable fpirit, for con-
tume'y and profcription. For God's fake! let
us ftand on the ground of the advantages we
poffefs, and leave the Americans to the bleffings
of independence!

I know it will be objected, that the Eaftern
provinces, depending much on their export to
the Weft Indies, on fhip building and the carrying trade, will be greatly diftreffed by the
meafure in queftion. To this I anfwer, that
as they no longer make a part of the Britifh
empire, it cannot be expected that we fhould
relieve *them*, by diftreffing *ourfelves*. Except in
the general interefts of humanity, what are
the diftreffes of the Eaftern provinces of America to us? They are certainly no more our
concern, than the Eaftern provinces of China
and Japan. Let their own government relieve
them out of their own refources.—Let France,
their moft favoured nation, relieve them.—Or
let them fhew England, that it is *her* intereft

to remove her reftrictions, by an adequate return
of benefit, and *fhe* will relieve them.—It is idle
to talk of gratuitous benefits in the intercourfe
of nations. The act fufpending the American
trade is therefore a meafure of juft policy, founded on a due regard to our commercial interefts.
It cannot be juftly conftrued into a meafure of
irritation, inafmuch as it fteers equally clear of
the intemperance of refentment, as of the folly
of unbalanced conceffion. It is an act that we
muft abide by, till the Americans concede fomething equivalent in return. The policy of Go-
tham would be difgraced, by adhering to the
ridiculous fpirit of *provifional reciprocity.* It
has already debafed us to the contempt of America, to the fcorn of our enemies, and to the
ridicule and pity of the reft of the world.

But another objection, much more ferious
in appearance, is that the act in queftion will
provoke a fpirit of retaliation in the New
States. The very turn of this objection difco-
vers the quarter whence it originates. If I rightly
underftand the term, *retaliation* prefuppofes an
aggreffion. Is there any aggreffion in regulating *our own trade?* But as there is a new fpecies of political *reciprocity*; fo, it feems, is there
a new kind of *retaliation,* now for the firft
time difcovered, for the purpofe of frighting
us from doing what it is plainly right and wife

in us to do. *Reciprocity* has coft us pretty dear. God forbid that *retaliation* fhould be equally chargeable !

But wherefore are we to be ftretched upon the rack of American retaliation ? Truly, be-caufe we will not admit the New States to a fhare, perhaps to the whole of the profits of our Weft India trade, in return for their ex-cluding us from their markets. They have been taught to connect ideas the moft diffimilar and irreconcileable;—they have been inftructed to affociate *independence* with *the advantages of Britifh fubjeEts.* The Britifh Weft Indies are not open to the Swedes, nor the Ruffians; wherefore is it that thefe nations do not threaten to *retaliate ?* They have a much better claim than independent America; they have not ad-mitted the fubjects of any other ftate to fuperior advantages in their ports. Will the New States *retaliate* on Spain, unlefs they are indulged with a free trade to the Spanifh main ? At this rate, there is to be no end to American *retaliation.* Or fhall we be told that the Englifh, who are the only people aggrieved by the tarif of the New States, are to be the only object of their *retali-ation,* unlefs they admit them to a participation, on their own terms, of a trade monopolifed by every other maritime nation ?

The

The demands of the New States are made pretty much after the following fashion. "We "have excluded you," says America, "from "every advantage of our past connection.— "You were a tyrant, no longer worthy our "favours—We have, besides, heaped calamity "upon your head, and loaded you with insult "—In return, you have secured to us, in per- "petual sovereignty, a fertile and extensive "territory, which, while subjects, we enjoyed "only in a disputed pretension---You have "granted to us your most valuable fishery--- "We have excluded you from ours---You have "granted us the fur trade, with the absolute "command of all the forts, lakes, rivers, and "carrying places, that are necessary to secure "its monopoly—We have requited you with "proscriptive duties—Concede to us a free "access to your West-India possessions, and "the carriage of your sugars to the European "market;—ship building is our trade; we, "therefore, can carry them cheaper than "*British-built* ships — Grant this, or we will "*retaliate*." — Better to perish with the little honour the peace has left us, than submit to such disgrace and humiliation from a *French* Congress, from *French* agents, and a confederacy of frantic committees!

But

But what are to be the dreaded effects of the juft refentments of their High Mightineffes the New States? *You will exafperate America to fuch a degree, that the whole of her trade will become an acceffion to France*---This is the idleft of all poffible fears ; the wideft from all rational theory on the fubject of commerce, as well as the moft contradictory of experience.

Commerce founded in a great meafure on imaginary wants, is as free of fpirit, and as independent of reftriction as the fafhions, opinions, and caprices of mankind. It may be fometimes moulded by much care and art, but it muft be guided with a pretty clofe conformity to its natural principles. Thefe principles are as various as the habits, cuftoms and fentiments of men, as diverfified as the climes they breathe in, and the countries they inhabit. Are thefe principles of commerce capable of being ftrained from their bias, by the arm of legiflative authority ?

Neither does the preference of the Americans reft merely on opinion. The fuperiority of Britifh manufacture, particularly of our woollens and hardware, fecures to us a confiderable fhare of the American trade. In the moft dreary period of the late war, it is well known, that Britifh manufactures forced their way to their

D   old

old market in the colonies, under every poffible difcouragement from the ruling powers. I
appeal to the experience of our merchants.
Has the trade increafed confiderably fince the cef-
fation of hoftilities ? By no neans. Thefe facts
are worth a thoufand fpeculations. They prove
in the moft forcible manner, the irrefiftible bias
of the American market to the Britifh trade.

No reftraints will be fufficiently efficacious
to extinguifh the deep-rooted predilection of the
Americans for articles of Britifh manufacture.
It is a fentiment founded on inveterate habits,
and upheld by a ftrong fenfe of convenience.
What then have we to fear from the paper
chains, with which the French have fettered the
American trade? On the firft pinch of reftraint,
the wily American will flip his neck from the
harnefs, and leave his *great* and *good* ally to
the idle condolements of *the council of the Am-
phyctions*. Britifh commerce with the ftrongeft
fibres, and the foundeft ftamina, is the moft
daftardly of cowards. The flighteft appearance
of competition and reftraint ferves to throw
this highly nervous fyftem into convulfions.
But the alarm foon wears off, and the native
vigour of its conftitution in a fhort time reftores
it to its natural health.

There

There is another circumſtance, that gives us an advantage above the French in the American market. The ſuperiority of his capital enables the Engliſh, to give a longer credit, than the French merchant. This circumſtance, ſo momentous in all commercial concerns, has a more powerful operation in America than elſewhere. There are few men of large fortunes in America, fewer than in any other country of equal population, and general opulence. It is a fact that in ſome of the northern provinces there are not two men, who can afford to ſpend a thouſand pounds a year out of their own country. The number of thoſe, who could cultivate their lands without an advance of many articles of European manufacture, was inconſiderable even before the war. They muſt have been reduced ſtill lower by their late exertions. It is unneceſſary to apply theſe remarks.

But ſuppoſe our miniſters to have every poſſible diſpoſition to conclude a commercial treaty with America, as I am fully perſuaded is the caſe, I would fain know, on what proſpect of permanence, it can be negociated in the preſent juncture? Not to mention the unnatural leaning of America to the intereſts of France, whoſe influence is now at its zenith, and will be hereafter hourly on the decline, what ſecurity can

we

we have, that the New States will carry into effect the ftipulations of their agents? Are their powers derived from Congrefs, or the provincial fovereignties? If from the firft, they will be difowned by the affemblies; if from the affemblies, they will be difregarded by the committees. There is no eftablifhed executive, at prefent in America — In the genuine fpirit of freedom, every man is his own governor. From Congrefs we can only expect the courtefy of recommendatory letters. Are the Britifh plenipotentiaries to pilgrim it from Penobfcot to Savannah, in fearch of the *reliques* of the *common fenfe of America?* Are they to conclude a feparate treaty, with every petty affociation, civil and military, which maintains an independent fovereignty within its refpective diftricts? *

The importance of the policy, proper to be obferved towards America, will fufficiently apologize for my having treated this fubject fo much in detail. The plan obferved by the prefent minifters, differs totally from that of their predeceffors. The former negotiated on the principle of exchanging fubftantial advantage, for fhadowy expectation. The latter, in the fpirit

* That there are men amongft us, who would favour a negociation of this kind, *their practices nearer home* fully evince —But that fuch practices will meet the approbation of men of integrity and independent principles, is an expectation, fomewhat too fanguine.

of plain dealing, are determined to give up nothing, that belongs to us, without an adequate
compenfation. Whether it be for the intereft
of this country to have a *commercial line* drawn
in the fpirit of Meff. Ofwald's *territorial bounda-
ry*, I leave to the difcernment of the reader.

Nothing, in my mind, can be equally efficacious to bring America to reafon, as the prefent ftrain of vigorous policy. To maintain
this, it is neceffary that Parliament fhould deci-
fively concur with the views of minifters. Let
us fhew the bold face of Unanimity, and a
ftable government to America, and fhe will
treat us with refpect and obfervance.

I am, in the next place, to proceed to examine
the new relations in which Holland ftands, as
well in refpect of this country, as of France.
In what manner the United States have become
an acceffion to our natural enemy, is not, I believe, fo generally known, as a matter of fuch
importance deferves. In order to have a clear
idea of this, as well as of the prefent difpofition
of the people of that country, it will be neceffary to look back to the ancient politics of the
ftates.

Soon after the eftablifhment of the Dutch
commonwealth, we read in their hiftory, that

it became divided into two powerful parties, which have subsisted ever since with little inter-mission—The one composed of, the friends and, adherents to the Prince of Orange—The other, consisting principally of the Aristocratic members of the commonwealth. The former is known by the name of the *Stadtholder*'s, the latter by that of the *Louvenstein Faction*. The Louvenstein party have ever been as warmly devoted to the French, as their adversaries to the English interest. There is a third party, called the Democratic, which is very considerable at all times, and at present carries with it a very great sway. This is the general outline of the state of parties in the Dutch commonwealth; there are several inferior subdivisions of interests, but they fall in with one, or other of the two great leading Factions.

But it is to be remarked, that the English interest has been often predominant, when the power of the Stadtholder has been at a very low ebb. Nor is the renovation of our ancient union with the States, at all connected, with the restitution of the prerogatives and former influence of the Stadtholder. This is a question of domestic policy, which it would be the extreme of folly, for Great Britain to intermeddle in, as she might thereby disgust some of her best friends, and still farther exasperate her enemies.

The

The democratic party has often fluctuated from one fide to the other. It is at prefent entirely French, and totally averfe from the Stadt-holder.

From the tragical termination of the power of the De Wittes, but more particularly from the time of the Revolution, to the commencement of the American war, the Englifh intereft had maintained a decifive afcendency — Yet the power of the Stadtholder had, in that long interval undergone many revolutions. The confolidating nature of commerce, which ferves to compact the principal maritime powers, into one great trading empire, partially jealous, but united in general intereft—A common jealoufy of the formidable growth of the power of France — joined with a cordial interchange of good offices—had cemented fo firmly the union between England and Holland, that it continued near a century unfhaken. It is reported of a great man, that he ufed to fay ; " *England and Holland were like man and wife, they might pout and wrangle; but it was their intereft not to part.*" We may confider them therefore at prefent, as in a ftate of temporary feparation *.

It feldom happens that the ties of natural affection, or political convenience, are diffolved

* Never were political, and matrimonial divorces more in vogue.

without the ill offices of third perfons. In the
prefent cafe, every engine of intrigue and cor-
ruption has been exerted on the part of France,
to detach the States from their connexion with
England. From the firft appearance of any
formidable fymptoms in the difcontents of America, the moft refined and unwearied policy was
employed by that power to fecure at leaft a
neutrality on the part of Holland in the pro-
jected attack on England. By a liberal and well
directed application of very confiderable fums
of money, the attachment of old friends was
fecured, and numerous profelytes were gained
over to favour the new fyftem. It is a notori-
ous fact, that a million of florins have been an-
nually appropriated for fome years back, to fecure the fingle province of Zealand to the
French intereft. Such arguments are powerful
in all countries—In Holland they are irrefiftible.
The event is known to all.

The leaders of the French faction, which at
prefent lords it without controul in the Dutch
councils, *are the grand penfionary, Van Guyzlaer, Zeebergen penfionary of Haerlem, and the
Capellans.* The character of *Van Berkel* is
well known. As to *Van Guyzlaer*, bold, turbulent and factious—Ambitious, fupple and un-
principled—He attaches himfelf indifferently to
any fet of men, and embraces, without fcrup'e,

any fyſtem of meaſures, which hold out the faireſt proſpect of gratification to his inſatiable appetite of power and emolument. The *Capellans* are violent popular leaders, who, by their virulent ſpeeches and publications have ſucceeded in inflaming the populace againſt England ; and in ſecuring the democratic weight to the Louvenſtein Faction.

From this brief ſketch of the preſent diſpoſitions of the Dutch, it is plain, that a long and intricate train of delicate policy is neceſſary on our part, in order to counteract the machinations of France, and reſtore Holland to her natural poſition. It requires a ſteady and vigorous hand to give her politics their true bias. From our friends every thing is to be expected, while we have at the head of affairs, a nobleman, connected by blood, principle and hereditary attachment, with the Engliſh intereſt in that country. But above all, a ſtrong and bold-faced adminiſtration, is requiſite to ſecure that degree of reſpect and confidence in this country, which alone can be effectual, to create that reſpect, which muſt ever be the baſis of all true friendſhip.

I am aware, it will be aſked—*Are the miniſters, who impoſed ſuch rigorous terms of peace, the pro-*

E   *per*

per *inftruments of conciliation with Holland?* *Are
they, who compelled the Ceffion of Negapatnam,
and wrefted from the Dutch a lucrative monopoly,
—aufpicious meffengers of harmony and friendfhip!*
To this I anfwer, that to give Holland a difguft for the French alliance, is the moft effectual meafure for fmoothing the way to a re-
union with that nation. Could any thing be
better calculated for this purpofe, than to fhew
the Dutch, by palpable experience, how groffly
they have been duped by that power who firft
involved them in an impolitic war, and after
multiplied loffes and difgraces, at the laft made
them the facrifice of an inglorious peace? This
objection is naturally made by thofe who agreed
to reftore Negapatnam and Trincomalé, that a
fpirit of uniform conceffion might be maintained
from the Miffiffippi to the Ganges. But, in the
name of Decency! let us hear no more of com-
plaint againft minifters, for fecuring to this poor
exhaufted country fome compenfation for her
mighty facrifices *.

I have

---

* Nothing can more ftrongly evince the folly and abfur-
dity of conceffion, when meant for the purpofe of conciliation, than an event, which has lately happened. An
Englifh nobleman of fome confequence in his country, who
had offered to the Dutch, *when he happened to be Minifter,*
Negapatnam with one hand, and Trincomalé with the
other,

I have now explained the double relations that both Holland and America ftand in, with refpect to Great Britain and France, in which we difcover difpofitions highly alarming to the former, and every way favourable to the atlter. We fee our friends and kindred deferting and fpurning us; we fee them united with our moft inveterate enemy to work our ruin. We fee both America and Holland rufhing madly from their fpheres, to take an unnatural pofition in the Houfe of Bourbon. The courage of the moft undaunted muft melt within him, in fuch a mighty convulfion of the political fyftem of the world. France, the center of all thefe prodigious commotions, has juft concluded a glorious and fuccefsful war, in all the pride of triumph, and with all the pomp of enlarged commerce, of extended territory, and of a flourifhing

other, and befides had feafoned the gift with all the fpices of the Eaft, in a late tour through the provinces, has met with a very ungrateful return for fuch unbounded liberality. The noble Lord hath himfelf announced to the public, that the only favour he had met with from this thanklefs people was barely — *that he was not torn in pieces by the m b.* Such is the difpofition of the Dutch populace to a *conceding* minifter—While the friends of England, which defcription comprehends almoft every man of high rank in the Dutch provinces, treated with a marked *coldnefs and diftruft, the bofom friend of the Comte de Vergennes.*

E 2   marine.

marine. Let us not weakly imagine, that the formidable confederacy, which but now menaced our deftruction, has been diffolved by the late pacification. The conjuncture is rendered more favourable, but its final diffolution, muft be effected by the united efforts of wifdom, unanimity, vigour and confidence. Should the difordered members of that overwhelming confederacy, be fuffered, without moleftation to acquire fhape and confiftency, under the plaftic influence of politic France, there is an end to the glories of the Britifh name—There is an end even to national fecurity. But I cannot be brought to think, that the independent gentlemen of England, will unite with the houfe of Bourbon — to weaken their country, by inteftine divifions—to difturb the repofe of their fovereign—and to blaft the credit and profperity of their country, by a capricious inftability, that muft inevitably reduce us to the mockery of the world. An honeft man will forget his little prejudices, at the call of public welfare — A great man will fubdue them, for the accomplifhment of a noble end, by the only practicable means.

It has been remarked of the people of England, that foreign war has been always efficacious, in quieting the rage of faction, and reftoring

ing

ing unanimity, and concert at home. If the wars of other times had this effect, how much more ftrongly ought the peace of the prefent to operate to the fame end ? Does any man living doubt, that the circumftances of the prefent peace, are more calamitous and alarming, than of any former war, except the laft, for a century paft ? If he does let him read the *preliminaries,* and look to the prefent ftate of foreign politics. Let him look to the navy of France — to the delufions of Holland, and the alienation of America. Let him afk Ruffia what her projects are? Whether her vaft ambition does not grafp the commerce of the Eaft, by opening the Cafpian and the Black feas, and fecuring the navigation of the rivers, that nearly connect them ? Afk the Emprefs whether her plan, be not to fecure that important trade, which poured the riches of the Eaft into ancient Pontus, and enabled Mithridates to make head for fo many years, againft the full braced vigour of the Romam arms? what will be the fate not only of that ineftimable commerce, but of every other branch of trade, fhould an active power, poffefs that vaft range of fertile territory, in which the indolent Muffulman repofes in his Haram, abounding with fuch opportunity of ports, and fuch conveniency of inland navigation, as fcarcely any
other

other country can boaft ? Befides the track by
the Cafpian, to the Northern and Eaftern parts
of India, will not the old trade with Hindoftan,
fo long enjoyed by the Soldans, and the Caliphs
by the Red Sea, and the ifthmus of Suez, be
once more attempted ? Thefe tracks are infi-
nitely fhorter, than that by the Cape of Good
Hope. Should thefe confiderations fail of conviction, I pronounce the underftanding of fuch
a man, an abject flave to faction, and his ftate
of political blindnefs utterly incurable. But my
hopes of *fuch* men are not very fanguine—It is
to the independent, the candid and difpaffionate
I addrefs myfelf—It is the remaining virtue of
the nation, which I adjure, by every thing dear
and valuable, which is left—by the honour and
fecurity of the State—by themfelves—their chil-
dren and pofterity—not to leave their country a
prey to civil Difcord, and the fport of deftroying
Faction.

But loud as is the call for unanimity, from
external emergency, the demands from internal
embarrafIment will be found equally urgent. I
am fully fenfible, that I am now to attempt a
very delicate tafk. If I fpeak freely of our domeftic politics, I may be thought, to prefs hard
on certain diftinguifhed characters, of weight
and

and confideration in the country. I have hitherto avoided, as much as poffible, all perfonal ftrictures. It is no longer in my power, to follow my private inclinations, without deferting the caufe of truth and the public. In this choice of difficulty, I think it better to hazard the indignation, even of perfons diftinguifhed by birth and power, than to leave any thing unfaid, which may ferve to inform the public mind, and enable the popular voice to utter the fentiments of truth and juftice. To fecure the cc-operation of the people in important fchemes of national utility, is an object of fuch confequence, that for the attainment of it, he muft be lukewarm in the public caufe, who will not run fome rifk. In the difcuffion, therefore, of queftions of internal policy, my duty to the public, obliges me to a neceffary franknefs, at the fame time that a regard to decency will enfure a proper degree of moderation and temperance. As my great object is to engage the united exertion of the nation by fetting before them the extreme urgency of our fituation, I fhall confine myfelf to fuch queftions, as create a general anxiety. In the firft rank of this defcription, ftand the affairs of the Eaft India Company.

The prefent alarming ftate, of the commercial and territorial concerns of the Britifh Company

pany trading to the Eaſt Indies, is an object of ſuch magnitude, as to deſerve the earlieſt atten-tion of Parliament. The abuſes in the govern-ment of the Company, both at home and a-broad—The heavy debts both to the public and individuals, incurred by a corporation, poſſeſ-ſed of an immenſe capital, at the head of the moſt lucrative monopoly in the world—The diſregard of legal authority by the proprietory at home, and the ſervants of the Company a-broad—all together beſpeak ſomething radically defective, in the conſtitution of the Company, which without a ſpeedy, and effectual cure from the ſeaſonable interference of parliament, muſt inevitably terminate, in a total diſſolution of its power and importance.

The obſervations, which I intend to make on the affairs of the Company, are meant to be bottomed on the authority of the reports and reſolutions, of the *Secret* and *Select Committees*. As it has become the practice to deny the credit of theſe documents, it therefore is requiſite, that I ſhould try to eſtabliſh their authority, before I proceed to ſtate facts, or deduce any reaſoning from their contents.

The Select Committee was appointed ſo long ſince as the year 1781, and has now ſat without

inter-

intermiffion for three entire feffions; in which
time it has brought forward a prodigious body
of evidence, which throws the fulleft light upon
the whole, and every part of this intricate and
complicated bufinefs.

This Committee is compofed of gentlemen of
the moft unfullied probity, and firft-rate talents,
whofe knowledge of the fubject cannot be queftioned, and whofe induftry and perfeverence are
only to be equalled by their candour and fair-
nefs—To diftinguifh individuals, without nam-
ing the whole, would be invidious.

The proceedings of this highly refpectable
Committee have been always open and public—
The teftimony of witneffes has been taken in the
moft folemn manner—The witneffes have been
many in number, and all of them poffeffed of
the fulleft knowledge on the points, to which
they have been examined—The moft material
evidence has been collected from the very perfons, who were principals or accomplices in
fome of the moft flagrant acts of delinquency.

So many circumftances, I believe, have never
before concurred to ftamp authority on the
proceedings of a Committee. A perfon would
think,

F

think, we were giving a logical detail of the conftituents of the higheft degree of credibility, inftead of the actual ftate of the Select Committee on India affairs, and its manner of proceeding.

Yet are the reports of a Committee fo conftituted, and proceeding in fuch an exemplary namner, daily libelled as groundlefs imputatations of unreal delinquency; and the members, who compofe it inceffantly traduced with the moft indecent fcurrility. But they have an enjoyment beyond the reach of detraction— They have the heart-felt confolation, of having done their duty to their country, by furnifhing a knowledge of the meafures, requifite to be adopted, in order to fave the Company from irretrievable bankruptcy, and to reftore to the wretched natives of India, the protection and fecurity of lawful government.

The refolutions brought forward by the Secret Committee, are a farther confirmation of the deference due to the reports of the Select Committee. There is fuch a precife coincidence of opinion between the refolutions of the Secret and the reports of the Select Committee, as nothing but the uniformity of conviction from the

the fame view of things, could have poffibly
produced. It were ridiculous to talk of a col-
lufion, between the members of the different
Committees, each in itfelf, and both compofed
of perfons differing on every other queftion of
policy. — Were they capable of fuch bafenefs,
they could have no poffible motive to induce
them to commit fuch a flagrant breach of the
high truft repofed in them.

There is therefore every degree of credit due
to the reports of the Select Committee, which the
clofeft inveftigation, aided by the moft unfuf-
pected teftimony, and a refpectable concurrence,
can confer upon the refult of parliamentary enquiry. Such is the folid foundation on which
I mean to ground my remarks. From this
evidence it will be made appear, that the corrupt
afcendancy of the Proprietory is the great fource
of all the diftreffes of the Company both at
home and abroad. For fake of clearnefs of
method, I fhall begin with a brief account of
their conduct under the operation of the act
of 1773.

The corruptions of the proprietory body, and
the infignificance of the Court of Directors, under
their controul, are fo fully fet forth, and au-
then-

thenticated in the Ninth Report of the Select Committee, that but little can be added to what is there faid. I fhall extract a few facts from that invaluable document, as fufficient for my prefent purpofe.

The firft is, the proceedings of the General Court on the charge brought againft Mr. Haftings, for having affifted, for a fum of money, to be paid to the Company, in extirpating the innocent nation of the Rohillas. On this charge Mr. Haftings was cenfured by the Court of Directors, who prepared an application to his Majefty for his recall. The General Court firft unanimoufly cenfured this meafure — In a fhort time after a majority of the proprietors fhewed a difpofition to approve the conduct of the governor, and refifted the application of the Court of Directors for his recall. This took place in the year 1775, when the regulating act of 1773 might be fuppofed to have had its full operation. A charge of peculation againft the governor was difmiffed at the fame time.

The next inftance of glaring partiality on the part of the proprietors to Mr. Haftings was in their *acquiefcing* to his continuing in the government of Bengal, after he had refigned, and

a fuca fucceffor had been nominated by the Court of Directors, and approved by the Crown.

I ftate thefe facts briefly without either comment or inference, as they have been already fo fully difcuffed in the Ninth Report. A governor-general of Bengal, who has the fuperintendance of an annual revenue of four millions fterling, which is double to what the whole revenue of England was in the reign of Charles II.—who has engroffed befides the whole vaft patronage of that kingdom, civil, financial and commercial, could not fail to find or *create* many advocates in a body conftituted on the plan of the proprietory — where money is power — and the conduct of individuals cannot be known from the practice of voting by ballot. Thus has the *felf-elected* and *felf-approved* governor of Bengal continued in his high ftation, unmolefted, except by fome faint murmurs of the Court of Directors.

The General Court, under the influence of the fervants of the Company, had now acquired an undifputed afcendancy over the Court of Directors. The next ftep was, to gain a victory equally decided over the authority of Parliament. Could this be accomplifhed, it was expected that

it

it would have completely eftablifhed the *independent fovereignty* of the governor and his General Court. The objeât was of fuch magnitude, as to deferve at leaft a vigorous attempt, which was made in the following manner.

On the authority of a moft refpeâable Committee, which had employed years in invefti- gating the ftate of the Company, a refolution paffed the Houfe of Commons, for the recall of Mr. Haftings. This alarmed the proprie- tory, who immediately affembled in General Court, and *ordered* the Court of Direâors, not to yield obedience to the vote of the Houfe of Commons.

The Court of Direâors were now divided be- tween the authority of Parliament, and the *commands* of the General Court. In order to extricate themfelves from this difficulty, a mid- dle courfe was refolved on. The Court of Di- reâors inftituted an enquiry of their own into the conduâ of Mr. Haftings. The refult of a long and laborious enquiry was to concur with the vote of the Houfe of Commons. This re- folution of the Court of Direâors brought matters to extremity.

A Ge-

A General Court was immediately convened, which without any form of enquiry, without examining a fingle witnefs, or calling for a fingle paper of any kind, after a fhort and tumultuous debate, inftantly refcinded the refolution of the Court of Directors, though backed by the authority of the Houfe of Commons; and though the whole executive power of the Company was vefted in the Court of Directors, by the regulating act of 1773.

Now was to be feen, to which of thefe authorities, the Court of Directors would yield obedience. That Court did not long continue in fufpenfe. The Directors had been fo long in a habit of implicit fubmiffion to the dictates of the General Court, conceiving themfelves bound by their refolutions, that they forthwith refcinded their order for the recall of Mr. Haftings, and prepared a letter to the governor to inform him of the fentiments of the proprietors.

While the nation was yet in amazement of this open defiance of all lawful authority, a new election of Directors came on. The General Court took this opportunity of manifefting ftill farther their utter contempt of the pro-

seedings

ceedings of Parliament ; and of profecuting their favourite plan of *independent fovereignty.*

Though the Court of Directors had fuffered themfelves to be overborne by menaces into an *acquiefcence* in the meafures of the General Court, they had not hitherto actively co-operated in the plan of the latter, of openly difclaiming all parliamentary authority. In order therefore to cement indiffolubly, all the parts of the independent Republic *governing* the Eaft Indies, in a firm compacted confederacy, under *one head*, they took advantage of the prefent opportunity, to raife to the Directory Mr. Sulivan, a perfon labouring under a parliamentary cenfure of delinquency in the government of the Company. This extraordinary meafure was accompanied with the elevation of others, to the fame truft, who had fhared deeply in the mifmanagement of the Company's affairs, and were warmly attached to the interefts of Mr. Haftings.

In this manner is an independent confederacy, attempted to be fet up in all the pride of Sovereignty, for the purpofe of plundering without controul or account the Britifh dominions in the Eaft. The Company is no longer a *commer-*

cial

cial corporation. It is a *political body* raised
on the ruins of commerce, and attentive only to
fhare in the rapine and peculation of thofe, who
are called the *Company's Servants,* but who are
in truth and fact the *Defpots of Afia.*

The Court of Proprietors is no longer compofed of individuals, who have thrown their
money into the Company's ftock, for the fake of
fharing in its *commercial* profits. The proprietory is made up of the friends, agents, dependents, and accomplices of the rulers abroad,
qualified by the fpoil, and attached by the patronage of Bengal. This ftate of the Company's
government calls loudly for the vigorous interpofition of Parliament, as well to refcue the
Legiflature from contempt, as to fecure the
trade of the nation, from the dreadful fhock,
which threatens every moment to overwhelm it.

This neceffity will appear in a ftronger light,
on a view of the conduct of the rulers abroad,
after they had completely new-modelled the conftitution of the Company at home.

Governor General Haftings, fecure of the
loyalty and obfequious attachment of his *faith-
ful Houfe of Proprietors,* began to difregard
G   the

the councils, and remonſtrances of *his privy council*, the Directors. Theſe remonſtrances were treated with contempt, left, as Mr. Bar-well tells us, they ſhould impair the *dignity of Mr. Haſtings' ſovereignty in the eyes of his ſubjeƐts.*

Salutary admonitions have been ever deemed ſubverſive of the *dignity of great princes*—This is an innate principle of royalty—Never was it more fully manifeſted than in the preſent in-ſtance—Never were the decrees of the Roman Senate, ſpurned with more contempt and haugh-ty averſion by Nero, or Caligula, than the orders of the Court of Directors have met with, from the *ſelf-throned ſovereign of Bengal.*

Next to refuſing good advice, the ſentiment moſt natural to a *mighty Prince*, is to extend his dominions by conqueſt. The *proprietory Emperor* of *Hindoſtan*, had the dazzling ex-amples, of Alexander and Tamerlane, before his eyes — Never has conquering ſpirit been more true to its principles — Never has it been more pompouſly attended with all its long and diſmal train of *exaƐions, oppreſſions, blood-ſhed, maſſacre, extirpation, peſtilence and famine.* His *ſubjeƐts* have been beggared to feed the war with ſupplies.

supplies. And some of the finest countries of the world have been desolated by the wild projects of his frantic ambition.

The *resources* of Mr. Hastings have been much extolled in the House of Commons and elsewhere. That the *friends* of the governor, have reason to speak with *rapture* of his *resources*, I make not the least question. With the *proprietors*, an increase of investment would at any time pass current for the extirpation of a whole people. But a discerning public can never be brought to consider with approbation, what is justly imputed to Mr. Hastings as the highest strain of delinquency. Even the proprietors would feel the effects of Mr. Hastings' *resources* in the failure of the investment of the present year, and the more than problematical danger of its never being revived to any valuable extent, in future, were they not in the habit of *other* compensations for the loss of *commercial profit*. Are we to thank Mr. Hastings, for exacting from the wretched natives of Bengal, a temporary supply to answer exigencies created by *his own* misconduct? Are we to thank him for the *plunder of imprisoned princes?* Are we to thank him for his *monopolies*, and exactions, which have exhausted every

source

source of future taxation and revenue? To what are owing, the ruin of trade—The rapid decrease of population — The decay of cultivation in the once flourishing kingdom of Bengal—The pride of Hindostan! and the granary of the East! To the *resources of* Mr. Hastings. — *Mr. Hastings' resources are* — *Beggary, ruin and extirpation.*

I know that certain persons have been in the habit of attributing the distresses and embarrassments of the Company's affairs to the war with France—I would ask these *advocates* for Mr. Hastings, whether the Mahratta war was owing to the rupture with France? Whether the irruption of Hyder Ally was owing to this cause? These wars are known to have been fomented by Mr. Hastings' treatment of the *native princes,* and his criminal projects of conquest. It is no longer doubtful, that the French armament was ordered to the East, in consequence of the tempting conjuncture, prepared by the policy of Mr. Hastings. Had it not been for the confederacy of the country powers, France would not have undertaken an expedition to a country, where she had not in possession a single port, town or fortress of any kind, nor so much territory, as might encamp a single company of soldiers.

To

To one only caufe are all our misfortunes in the eaft to be imputed. They have originated folely and exclufively from the wild ambition of *one* man, fupported by a corrupt confederacy at home, unchecked by directorial or parliamentary controul.

The evil is at length brought home to the feeling of the public. The wound given to the refources of the Company's commerce, is felt to the quick in the revenues of the ftate. The payment of the duties on their imports is obliged to be fufpended. The debts due by the Company, to the nation, and private perfons, without any reafonable profpect of being able to pay them, are very *confiderable.**

Inftead

---

* The following is a ftatement of the debts, incurred and due by the Company at home.

Eaft-India debt in England.

	£.
To the cuftoms — —	100,000
To freight and demorage — —	294,704
To freight and demorage —	324,000
To bills of exchange — —	2,460,000
To goods and ftores exported —	160,969
To fundry articles in the department of the committee exclufive of export —	20,750
To warrants paffed the courts unpaid	87,700
To fupra cargoes commiffion — —	7,559

To

Inftead of the Bengal inveftment ftanding in the high fcale of a million fterling, the Company is reduced to borrow that fum from her own fervants, at an intereft of eight per cent. to fupply the inveftment of the prefent year. Inftead of fleets crouding our ports freighted with the precious commodities of the Eaft, the property of Britifh merchants ; we have now nothing left, but the importation of the fortunes of fplendid delinquents, amaffed by peculation, and rapine. Even this miferable traffic muft fhortly have an end, as there is nothing left for farther depredation. As foon as the Governor General and the creatures of his power, have invefted the whole of their ill-gotten wealth in returns from Bengal, *at a profit of eight per cent.*; in the pre-

To money borrowed at the Bank with 4 per cent intereft thereon —	284,523
To proprietors of private trade —	53,000
To intereft on annuities — —	46,011
To intereft on bonds ——	41,300
To dividends on ftock — —	63,849
Total Englifh debt —	£. 4,574,370

The whole making above four millions and a half of Englifh debt. Where is the fund to difcharge this vaft debt ? Why are the *proprietors of Eaft-India ftock* the only perfons in the nation who do not tremble at the confequences ?

fent

fent courfe of things, there muft be a final ftop
to the trade with that kingdom.

The extreme urgency of legiflative interpofition, in order to fave the Company from irretrievable bankruptcy, and the nation from fuch
a mighty lofs of trade and revenue, as muft be
confecuent thereon, is, I believe fufficiently
eftablifhed. The next confideration is the nature of the remedy to be applied. Nothing, in
my opinion, will be found effectual to this end,
fhort of an entire reform of the conftitution of
the Company. It is neceffary to wreft the
trade from the hands of *politicians*, and to re-
eftablifh it firmly on *commercial principles*.

· Whether it be at all expedient to delegate to
a company of merchants, fuch extenfive *fovereign powers*, as are neceffary for the government of a vaft extent of populous territory, at
fuch an immenfe diftance from the feat of power,
is a queftion, which has been already much agitated. It is a queftion of fuch magnitude and
importance as to deferve a much abler confideration, than any I can give it. However I cannot help obferving, that the circumftances of
the times, if not the unalterable relations of
things, would juftify, a much more coercive
and

and extended executive, and legiflative controul, if not the entire affumption of both, in the territorial concerns of the Company. The abftract queftion of right, though evidently favourable to fuch a meafure, goes but a little way towards a decifion of the point. It is upon the folid ground of permanent advantage to the Company, and the nation, that the meafure fhould be finally decided.

If a *high-handed* government, as fome have faid, be neceflary for the adminiftration of our eaftern dominions, a *high-handed* executive at home, is indifpenfably neceflary for the controul of fuch a government. If it be neceflary to arm the reprefentative of the Britifh power in the eaft, with great prerogatives, and an extenfive difcretion, a magiftrate cloathed with fuch high command, fhould be obliged to yield the moft implicit fubmiffion to orders from home. No fufpenfions, no qualifications, no compromife, fhould be admitted in refpect of the pofitive orders of his fuperiors. Much lefs, fhould a contumacious difobedience, on principle, be a moment tolerated. Whether it be poffible to give to a company of merchants, or if poffible, whether it be wife, to confer fuch *formidable powers* on *fubjects,* deferves a very ferious confideration.

To

To me I own it feems *impoffible* to confer on
a body of merchants, whofe capital falls far
fhort of the revenue of the country, which
they are to govern, fuch an efficient authority,
as will not be eluded It is a maxim in both
the natural and moral world, that the acceffory
follows the principal. A Governor General of
Bengal adminiftering a revenue of four millions, will 'till human nature undergoes a total
change, inevitably gain an entire afcendancy
over a company of merchants, dividing a few
hundred thoufand pounds. Thus it is evident
that by attempting a weak and inadequate remedy, the evil of the prefent day will recur
upon us every ten or dozen years.

A *commercial* company will not complain of
fuch a meafure. Trade has become a bankrupt,
by the expenfive fellowfhip of fovereignty —
It has flourifhed as a private citizen — The me-
retricious blandifhments of power will ever
bring ruin on a merchant — Commerce cannot
repofe with fafety in her arms.

But whatever the ftrength of the fpecific may
be, which the wifdom of Parliament may think
proper to adminifter, for the cure of the prefent
diftemper, the difficulties infeparable from the ap-

H   plication,

plication, are eafily forefeen. They arife from the delirious ftate of the patient; from the oppofition of the cuftodees of the eftate; and from the numerous tribe of legacy hunters, who expect large bequefts of power and emolument, on the demife of the commerce and credit of their country. Clamour without doors, and a vigorous oppofition within, muft be refolutely encountered.

The trumpet of Bengal has long fince founded the alarm of danger. From the very firft inftitution of an enquiry, a light body of irregulars, were ordered to watch the enemy, and throw every poffible impediment, in the way of inveftigation. As the danger has increafed, their force has been gradually augmented. Their activity of late has been redoubled, fo that fcarce a day revolves, without bringing with it, a periodical return of abufe, againft the characters and proceedings of the inquifitorial members.

Thefe active troops combat with the defperation of men, whofe exiftence is at ftake. The wealth of Bengal has been liberally applied to fructify the prefs. Should the trade of Nabob-making be radically deftroyed, the numerous body of veteran literati, will meet with as little en-

encouragement, as the *artifts of Dacca have re-ceived from the Britifh government.* Billinf-gate *and St. Giles's will become as defolate, as the Carnatic, fhould Mr. Haftings be recalled.* What mercy then could the hardy man expect, who firft ventured to draw the veil, and, expofe to public view *the fcorpion feet of Indian de-linquency.**

But it is not from the praife-worthy zeal of men, combating *pro aris & focis,* that you are to meet with the moft formidable oppofition. Speak of the delinquency of Mr. Haftings in the Com-mons — You inftantly draw upon you the whole cry of his clamorous dependents. *Where is Mr. Haftings proved a delinquent? Will you condemn an abfent man? Mr. Haftings' delinquency is recorded in the Reports of the Committee of Par-liament — In the corruptions of the Proprietory — In the debility of the Directors — In the contempt of Parliament — Mr. Haftings' delinquency! — Heaven and Earth! — Mr. Haftings' delin-quency! — Does any man living doubt it? It is marked in the bankruptcy of the Company — in the difgrace of the Britifh name — and in the defolation of the fourth part of the world.*

* *But little, indeed, has been fhewn by the exafperated corps — fave that they have not been hitherto fo malicious as to praife him.*

Thofe

Thofe men, who call for other *proofs* of Mr. Haftings' guilt, don't confider the difference of evidence, that is neceffary to convict in a court of juftice, from that requifite to bring home criminality to a great executive magiftrate. But the general fenfe of mankind will tell them, that, where charges of heinous offences are impu ed, in the moft folemn manner, before a competent tribunal, to a magiftrate in high truft and extenfive command, fuch imputation is a fufficient proof of delinquency, unlefs it be fairly met and fully refuted. It is not a fufficient caufe, for continuing a Governor General in the defpotic command of Afia, that he may poffibly efcape the legal penalties of a conviction at the Old Bailey. The character of a magiftrate in fuch high truft, fhould be chafte, it fhould be free from even colourable imputations. Nothing in my mind more ftrongly evinces the radical deficiency of the conftitution of the Company, than the circumftance of our being obliged to call the enormities of Mr. Haftings, by the gentle name of *delinquency.* 'Till offences of fuch magnitude come under the legal defcription of *overt acts of treafon and felony, or of fome more general term, comprehending every fpecies of both,* we can have no fufficient fecurity for the obedience or upright demeanour of a Governor General of Bengal. --- As to his *abfence,* it cannot

cannot be fairly made ufe of by his advocates, as a plea of innocence, as every effort has been made by Parliament, to procure an opportunity of confronting him with his accufers. Had *Verres* continued in Sicily during his whole life, he might on the fame plea, have been held out to the Romans, as *an innocent, calumniated man.*

But who is *Mr. Haftings*, who has braved for fuch a length of time, the united force of the whole legiflature? Can any thing more forcibly evince to the apprehenfion of the public, how deeply the evil has taken root, than the difficulty not of punifhing, but bringing to a trial this overgrown offender? *The whole executive, and a confiderable part of the legiflative powers of the State, have been exerting their utmoft force for years without effect, in order to dethrone Mr Haftings;* — the difgraceful conteft is yet in fufpence *.

The neceffity of a vigorous exertion of the whole legiflature is all that is now requifite to effect a complete and fubftantial reform. The labours of the committees have furnifhed the

* Thofe who decry the credit of parliamentary enquiry would reduce the Houfe of Commons, to a very abject ftate. By wrefting from that Auguft Affembly, its inquifitorial priviliges, you deprive it of all power either of protecting its friends, or annoying its enemies.

most

most ample materials for the information of Parliament. The zealous support of men of independent principles and fortunes, alone is necessary. Government, on the India business, may possibly be deserted by several, who are in the habit of co-operating with it on other occasions. Should the independent members unite with the *present malecontents*, and those interested in the present destructive system, the fate of this great question will be highly precarious. The vast importance of the objects to be secured by decisive measures, must be a strong incentive to secure the co-operation of every honest and disinterested man. The security of our Asiatic trade and dominions — the safety of a million and a half of the national revenue, which depends on this trade—but above all the happiness, and protection of the miserable natives of India call loudly, on the national justice and wisdom, for a manly and substantial reformation.

The very critical situation of the affairs of Ireland is another object, that must necessarily claim a great share, of the attention of ministers, and in some shape or other be brought before Parliament in the course of the session; most probably by those who wish to take occasion from thence to embarrass government, and forward their own views and interests. I do

not

not mean to give an opinion on the political
meafures, which are at prefent purfuing by the
natives of that kingdom, nor of the propriety of
the mode, by which they are attempted to be carried into effect. England fhould avoid at all times
making herfelf a party in the domeftic politics
of her neighbours. As long as the Irifh fhew
the fame hearty difpofition, to adhere to the
fpirit and letter of the union, fo indifpenfable to
the interefts of both countries, on the footing,
on which in conformity to their repeated re-
quifitions, it has been lately fettled, the Parliament of England can have neither pretence nor in-
ducement to interfere in their conftitutional concerns.

That there is not the fmalleft intention on the
part of Ireland to depart in the minuteft particu-
lar from their late folemn compact, does not admit of the leaft queftion. What I fhall fay on
the fubject, therefore, is not meant to imply the
flighteft doubt of the fincere attachment of the
Irifh to this country. On the contrary it will
prove, that their loyalty to their Sovereign, and
affection to England, are not to be fhaken by
all the artful induftry of mifreprefentation and
mifconftruction. Ireland is too grateful for the
benefits lately received, not to feel a frefh ala-
crity in the caufe of Great Britain. She is too
wife,

wife, not to difcern that the attempts of men, *fore from difappointment*, are meant to foment national jealoufies and difcontents, ruinous to both countries. The Irifh muft recollect with gratitude, and repay with confidence, the uniform and confiftent conduct, of many perfons, who compofe the prefent adminiftration, on every queftion relating to their trade and conftitution. In every change of fortune, they have held the fame countenance to Ireland. In their adverfity they have not flattered her, nor have they looked cold on her in their profperity. At this moment they are defirous of complying with every demand, confiftent with the welfare of both countries; more the moderation of Ireland will not infift on.

That the moft intimate fœderal union between the fifter kingdoms, is neceffary to the welfare and profperity of both, is a truth fo obvious, that it were an idle wafte of time, to attempt to prove it. But the conclufions, generated by this undifputed propofition, are worthy the moft ferious confideration. If the prefervation of the prefent connexion, be effential to the interefts of Great Britain and Ireland, the means of ftrengthening the ties, which brace this connexion, muft be highly important. To me, I own, a

govern-

government refpectable in ftrength, and credit-
able in its component parts, feems abfolutely requifite to this end.   It follows that every attempt to diminifh the refpectability, and weaken
the force of government, in either country, aims
a mortal wound againft the vital principle
of the fubfifting connexion *.   If in the prefent
ftate of things, when the minds of men are but
little difpofed to adhere to what is known and
cuftomary, and ·the moft paffionate attachment
is difcovered for whatever is new and uncommon——If, during the continuance of this diftem-
pered appetite of the human mind, which loaths
the plain and wholefome food, that has hitherto
nourifhed political opinions and conftitutiorial
principles, and requires to be daily pampered
with any endlefs variety of new projects, and
frefh theories :   If, in the very crifis of innovation, a difguft fhould be given of lawful government, through the abufes of a weak and
fluctuating adminiftration, confequences the moft
tremendous may be expected.

* *A noble Lord,* who held a diftinguifhed ftation in Ireland, is accufed of having fplit the force of the Crown in
· that country into numerous divifions and fubdivifions, of
his *family connexions,* and *perfonal friends*—If this charge be
founded, the noble Lord ftands impeachable of the higheft
ftrain or delinquency, which was poffible to be committed
by a Viceroy, in the prefent critical fituaticn of that
country.

I   This

This confideration does not feem to have had its due weight with thofe refpeƈtable charaƈters, whofe correfpondence with the volunteers has lately appeared in *all the daily papers*. Where they were afked their opinions relative to a great conftitutional queftion, it might have been deemed wife, not to have introduced into their anfwers, *allufions* to *things and perfons*, totally independent of the merits of the propofition to be difcuffed. It can make no difference on earth to the fuccefs of a parliamentary reform, either here or in Ireland, whether the Duke of Portland, or Lord Temple, Lord North, or Lord Thurlow have a fway in the councils of his Majefty—Their fentiments on this, if on no other queftion, are perfeƈtly unanimous. Therefore as nothing favourable to the caufe of reprefentation could be inferred from a change of adminiftration, all cenfure of the prefent government muft have had in view *other* objeƈts, befides the event of that queftion. I can fcarcely fufpeƈt perfons of high rank and diftinƈtion in the country, of an *intention* to inflame the difcontents, if any there be, in the fifter kingdom. But moft certainly it was imprudent to let any thing fall which might tend to exafperate, where temper and confidence are fo highly neceffary. Befides the mifchief of thefe unfeafonable allu-

fions,

fions, the glaring contradictions, with which their plans of reform abound, is a circumftance highly unfavourable to the credit of this country. It may teach the volunteers to have a very contemptible opinion of the underftanding of a nation, whofe good fenfe they once refpected, to find that the great and diftinguifhed characters, whom they looked up to, as the Britifh Solons * of the day, have furnifhed them with theories of reform, which are complete anfwers to each other. The volunteers have already manifefted a decreafe of refpect for the fpeculations of Britifh reformers †. They complain, that when they confulted Britifh legiflators, *about the mode of reforming their Parliament*, they were anfwered by a *confiftent* Philippic on the prefent adminiftration, in which all agreed; and an *inconfiftent* digeft of reforming crofs purpofes, where they

---

* The Duke of Richmond and Doctor Price, Mr. Pitt and Dr. Jebb, Lord Effingham and Mr. Wyvil, have given in fix *different plans of Parliamentary Reform*—Each is declared by its author to contain the only changes worth contending for.

† The Duke of Richmond's *fimple* plan of extending the Right of Suffrage to every man in Ireland, and finifhing the elections on one day, has been very indecently treated in the Provincial Affembly of Leinfter. It was fcouted, as giving the whole power of election to the mob, exclufive of fome little difficulties in reducing it to practice.

are all at variance. Can the towering ſtructure of parliamentary purity, whoſe ſummit is meant to touch the ſkies, be poſſibly raiſed, in ſuch a confuſion of languages?

The Iriſh are a diſcerning people, quick-ſighted in tracing the ſprings of political action. It muſt of courſe have infuſed into the minds of that people, no ſmall degree of jealouſy and ſuſpicion, in regard of *Engliſh profeſſions,* to obſerve the microſcopic acuteneſs, with which certain men,* who never manifeſted the ſmalleſt attention to the intereſts of Ireland, while they had the ability to ſerve her, *now* diſcover in the meaſures of the *preſent* government, principles, imperceptible to general apprehenſion, *which muſt neceſſarily create tumult and diſorder in that country.* The laviſh encomiums *now* beſtowed on the volunteers by perſons, who formerly treated them with the moſt marked contempt, is another circumſtance, which muſt have a tendency to depreciate the currency of *Engliſh profeſſion.* †

Where

* Witneſs Lord Thurlow's treatment of Mr. Townſhend's bill for quieting the diſcontents in Ireland. And the noble Lord's *unparallelled* argument on the Dominica bill.

† Lord Shelburne was heard in his place in the Britiſh Houſe of Lords, in the face of his country, to honour the

Where there are fo many caufes to weaken the national credit with the inhabitants of Ireland, it is highly neceffary to give every poffible affiftance to the meafures of government, which are intended to conciliate the confidence of that people, and cultivate the benefits of the prefent connexion. As much as the character of the nation, muft have neceffarily fuffered from the infincerity of private complaifance, in the fame proportion is it neceffary to exalt the credit of the Britifh government, left the Irifh fhould, from the late *unfavourable fpecimens*, think us, a faithlefs, chimerical, and timeferving people, utterly regardlefs of every conftitutional as well as commercial queftion, which does not lead directly or indirectly to power and emolument.

I have now gone through the whole of what I propofed, at my outfet, to detail in this concife review of the ftate of the nation, in which, I think, I have fully evinced the neceffity there is for a comparéd, vigorous, and decided government. But as my plan may be deemed imperfect, without faying a few words on the man-

volunteers with the name of " *an armed mob*" — Yet the noble Lord *now deputes* Doctor Price to *calculate a panegyric on the virtues of this* — *armed mob*. —

ner,

ner, in which fuch a government *ought* to be conftituted, I muft beg leave to trefpafs a little longer on the patience of the reader.

Parties, whether generally more beneficial or prejudicial, are allowed to be infeparable from the politics of a free ftate. It is therefore of the higheft importance to the national welfare, that they be fo managed, as that the greateft poffible good may be derived from them, with the fmalleft poffible inconvenience. In order to fee, how this may be beft done in the prefent juncture, it will be neceffary, to look pretty far back into the ftate of parties.

The two great parties, which have fubfifted in this country near a century, were marked at firft with the wideft line of difcrimination of views and principles. The prerogatives of the crown, was the great ground, on which this line of difference was firft drawn. Ever fince the Revolution, the firft diftinctions have been gradually difappearing, while others have infenfibly fprung up in their place. The two parties however ftill retained their ancient names, though their principles and opinions had undergone an almoft total change. *Whig* and *Tory* ftill continued to be bandied about, as the well known

known words of political rendezvouz, though
the latter had long deferted the weak and un-
tenable ground of *prerogative*, and filently taken
poft behind the covert-way of *influence*. But
as the change was gradual, and in the natural
courfe of things ; and entirely confiftent with
the fpirit of firft principles, the confequences
were not at all difadvantageous to the interefts
of the public.

Things continued in this natural ftate of pro-
greffion, from the Revolution to the commencement of the prefent reign. Then was begun
the work of a new fyftem, totally different
from the conftitution and end of both the parties, which had hitherto divided the nation.
The influence of the crown, inftead of being
employed, as hitherto had been ufual, in giving
afcendancy to one or other of the leading parties; or in bracing the vigour of a coalition of
both, in trying emergencies; was now, for the
firft time, exerted with the impracticable aim of
diffolving all parties, and abolifhing for ever
the national diftinctions of Whig and Tory —
What effect this plan muft have had will be
learned by looking a little into the nature of
party.

Party

Party is defined by Mr. Locke to be, *A num-*
ber of perfons confederated by a fimilarity of de-
figns and opinions, in oppofition to others. Now
it obvioufly appears from this definition, which
muft be acknowledged to be a juft one, that
parties can only be deftroyed by rendering a
fimilarity of defigns and opinions univerfal, or
by preventing all confederacy between men of
fimilar principles. The flighteft knowledge of
human nature evinces the impracticability of
removing parties in the former way; the latter, therefore, is the only means by which
their removal can be effected. The principle,
confequently, of the new fyftem, which had in
view the extinction of all parties, muft have
been the deftruction of every bond of union,
by which men are united in a *fimilarity of po-*
litical defigns and opinions.

The defign was to appearance fpecious and
plaufible, as almoft every new theory in government is, on a fuperficial obfervation. The
evils of *party* were known, and had been often
felt. it was therefore highly gratifying to public
expectation, to hold out a profpect of entirely
removing them. The popularity of the new plan,
and its fpecious plaufibility, were taken advantage of by thofe who had the honour of fharing
the

the Royal confidence, to fecure the approbation of a youthful, liberal-minded, fanguine Prince, highly defirous of manifefting his ardent attachment to his people by new and uncommon inftances of grace and favour.

Trial therefore was made of the new theory. Then it appeared that in the ardor of the benevolent difpofitions of the Sovereign, and amid the fond delufion of national hope, the moft ordinary maxims of political wifdom had been entirely overlooked. It was not forefeen, that nothing fhort of abfolute defpotifm could fupply the lofs of that energy and vigour, which neceffarily attend on a *fimilarity of defigns and opinions.*

The confequences were exactly, what might have been fore-known, did the tumult of innovation admit of a moment's reflexion. A fyftem of court cabal and political intrigue, was fubftituted in the place of the open and manly fpirit, which had hitherto characterifed the Britifh monarchy. Divifion, weaknefs and treachery were introduced on principle, in the place of union, ftrength and good faith. The ancient parties were confounded and difordered by the attacks of this irregular enemy, who without

K   coming

coming to a decisive action, like the ancient British charioteers, incessantly harrassed the heavy
bodies of political confederacy. The Tories
as being less firmly compacted were entirely
broken and dispersed. The Whigs made a long
and desperate stand, but were at last disordered
and obliged to quit the field.

The enemy now fully triumphant was left to
his own plans and schemes of policy. Self-
government is sure destruction to a lunatic.
Discontents, disorders and tumults at home,
weakness, pusillanimity and contempt abroad,
were the first fruits of the new system.

The character of one of the most amiable
princes, that ever lived, was exhibited to his
subjects through a medium the most unfavourable to his numerous virtues. The Sovereign
was represented to his people, as the patron of
treachery, and the rewarder of desertion of
friends and abandonment of principle. His
royal dignity was impaired by the low intrigues
and despicable cabals which surrounded his
throne. His repose was hourly interrupted by
the murmurs of his people, and the petty
wrangles of men, who having purchased wealth
and power, by the sacrifice of character and
honour,

honour, naturally quarrelled about the divifion of the fpoil. *Even the facred perfon of a Britifh King* was not exempted from the moft un-parallelled outrage, from the venal and flagitious wretches, who were the creatures of the new fyftem. This circumftance is the more remarkable, as this defcription of men, affumed to themfelves the honourable appellation of *King's friends*; and now affect to treat with abhorrence the fmalleft *parliamentary* refiftance to the will of the fovereign.

The fame fpirit, which proceeded to fuch unprecedented enormities at home, was foon introduced into the adminiftration of the diftant parts of the empire. Our oldeft and beft friends, our neareft kindred, could no longer difcern the ancient plainnefs and native honour of the Britifh character, under the unnatural veil of artifice, infincerity and intrigue. The *Britifh parties* were diffolved, but the *Britifh character* was no where difcoverable in the national government.

Hence all the multiplied calamities and difgraces of the prefent reign — Hence the mighty loffes of trade and territory, under which the nation is at this moment finking. This fyftem

has

has achieved in the short space of twenty years, what prerogative failed to accomplish in a hundred — What influence had been labouring near a century in vain. What the united force of the power and policy of the house of Bourbon could not accomplish, a system of disunion has effected. In the course of a few years of licentious policy, this system has weakened the force — diminished the resources — and degraded the character of the British nation. Ask the cause of the dismemberment of the empire, and the rapid strides of national depression and ruin? You are answered — They *are owing to the system of national division.* What has defaced the glories of the British name, and shaken the relations of the universe? *The system of division.* It has done all of ruin, disgrace and humiliation, that it was possible for it to do — It has contrasted the æras of *sixty* and of *eighty-three* — But *it has not extinguished the invincible vigour of the British spirit.*

On the remains of *this spirit*, on the great principle of resistance to this overwhelming system — the abyss of dominion and commerce — Is the present coalition of parties founded—The principle of support or resistance to this *system* is the true line of discrimination, that separates the parties, which at present divide the nation.

All

All the parties in the kingdom were broken and frittered into infignificance. Deferters from every denomination and defcription of men had taken a part in the new-confirructed government, as intereft and inconftancy had prompted. The eyes of the nation were now fully open. ed to its deftructive tendency — Whig and Tory exifted but in name — They were ranged promifcuoufly under the banners of the common enemy — Nothing was left from which relief could be expected, *but a renewal of confederacy on the ancient principles of the conftitution.*

What is whiggifm? Is it not the native vigour of the Britifh fpirit, refifting whatever is found practically dangerous to the liberties and profperity of the nation? If this be not whiggifm, it is fomething that does not deferve to be explained, it is a fpirit which fhould have never exifted — But that this *is* the fpirit of whiggifm can be eafily evinced from its exertions in the caufe of the conftitution.

This fpirit has undergone three great changes within a century. It oppofed *prerogative,* as long as it was dangerous to the rights and liberties of the fubject — When *prerogative* was no longer formidable, and *influence* became

alarming,

alarming, the *British spirit* resisted its progress —
At present the spirit of whiggism is up in arms
against an enemy more formidable than both
influence and prerogative united.

The bond of union, which unites all, who
deserve the name of *Whigs*, is a principle of resistance, to whatever threatens the constitution
and welfare of the state — Let us reason of
things, not of names — Is not this the bond
of the *present coalition?* Their bond of union is
not the antiquated maxims, which anciently
united the Whigs of former times — It is a new
necessity grown up within the memory of man —
The impression is varied, but the bullion is the
same — It is the ancient unbroken spirit of the
British nation, which has triumphed on the
ruins of the late system —

I am prepared for the little cavils of little
men — *Is Lord North a Whig?* I will not re-
tort this idle petulance, though I have such
ample scope — But I would ask a seceding Whig,
I respect the character, though under the temporary influence of delusion and error — Was
not something to be relinquished by a virtuous
citizen for the salvation of his country? Was
the

[71]

the *Revolution* effected without a coalition of
Whigs and Tories?

It is remarked by an elegant and judicious
writer, that the generality of people are half
a century behind-hand in their politics — Fatal
will it be to our liberties, and remaining power
and trade, fhould the Englifh nation, in the
prefent juncture, furnifh an additional example
of the truth of this maxim. The nnmerous
abettors of the *late fyftem* are ftill in force.
Several of the moft refpectable Whigs in the
nation have been for a while mifled by the
founds of ancient names. They mean honeftly,
but they are bewildered in the puzzle of diftinctions, which exift no longer.

I entreat thefe men to look narrowly into the
actual ftate of *parties*, and to examine the real
fituation of things. It is not in the depreffion,
but the revival of *parties, conftructed on the
fpirit of ancient principles, that we are to feek
the renovation of Britifh honour and profperity.*
The only queftion at prefent is, whether thofe
who endeavour to reftore the ancient ftate of
things under which the nation flourifhed for a
century, are to be preferred to perfons, who
feek to renew a *fyftem*, which in the fpace of
twenty

twenty years, has reduced us from the most flourishing to our present most miserable state— It is not a little question of *station and emolument*—But a great and eventful question of *system*—It is not the cause of *men*, but of *principle* —which is now at hazard —

Οἴη πὲρ φύλλων γενεὴ, τοιήδε καὶ ἀνδρων.

Like leaves on trees the race of man is found,
Now green in youth, now withering on the ground.
                                                    POPE.

Men and their interests pass away --- But principle strikes root, and outlives many successive generations of politicians --- *I implore the seceding whigs, by their former virtuous struggles — By the honours of their progenitors — By the revered cause of whiggism for which their ancestors have fought and bled — I adjure them by the miseries of their country — and the distresses with which she is encompassed — not to aid in restoring that desolating system, which required the whole united force of the nation to push it from its basis.*

The nation has begun already to taste the fruits of union and vigour in her councils. Every thing has been done by the present administra-
                                                    tion,

tion, which could have been expected from it. They have rectified, as far as it was poſſible to rectify, the blunders, and inaccuracies of the Preliminaries --- They have corrected their pernicious tendency, where it was practicable, without a breach of *public faith.* They have obtained for the nation ſome compenſation for it's loſſes by the favourable terms with the Dutch, and thereby have given a degree of eclat to the iſſue of a calamitous war, and of a peace, ſtill more calamitous. But above all they are *united* within themſelves, and poſſeſſed of the confidence of Parliament. If we look to the *conſtitution* of the preſent miniſtry, it is compoſed, as every adminiſtration in this country ſhould be, of *a coalition* of talents, experience, property and character — Its *conſtitution* deſerves confidence, and the *principles*, on which it has acted hitherto, ought to inſure it.

It is no juſt objection to the *conſtitution* of the preſent miniſtry, that the paſſions, prejudices and intereſts of men have a ſhare in it --- What human inſtitution was ever entirely free from them? If they are known to influence the abſtracted purity of religious faith, how can the ſoundeſt political principles be expected to eſcape the common lot of human opinion? *May I periſh the day, when*

L   *I ſtand*

I stand up the advocate of an administration, formed on unconstitutional principles! The very charges, which by its enemies are daily urged against the coalition, prove the soundness of the *principle*, on which it is bottomed. The most aggravating imputation brought against it, is that it is a *formidable aristocracy*, cemented with such strength and consistency, that no power in the nation can resist it. From William to George the Third has any man employed either his tongue or his pen against a *whig* administration, who did not make use of a similar argument? In short, look to the *principle, the conduct*, or the *sins* of the coalition---You every where discern the genuine features of *whiggism.*

Let us now look to the *candidates for power*, and what do we see to tempt us to transfer our confidence from its present objects? We meet with a mass of discontent, composed of parts so very heterogeneous, that they agree in one thing only—namely, the pursuit of revenge and ambition, by any means, and at every hazard. Are we to expect from such a heap of contradictions, fermented by the ancient leven of *systematic discord*, a stable and permanent government? What success can the nation expect to any of the important schemes of policy now in agita-

agitation from an adminiftration fo whimfically conftituted? What can the *Sovereign*, what can the *people* expeét from a revival of the *late fyftem?* Contempt abroad, and diftraétions at home muft be the firft fruits of power fo conferred — *Without concert, without charac- ter, without popular favour, without Parlia- mentary fubport, or the Royal confidence — the adminiftration of fuch men, conftituted on fuch principles, MUST INEVITABLY LEAD TO SOME difmal convulfion, financial or commer- cial.*

T H E   E N D.